THE STAR HUSBAND

THE STAR HUSBAND

by Jane Mobley

illustrated by Anna Vojtech

DOUBLEDAY & COMPANY, INC. GARDEN CITY, NEW YORK

ISBN 0-385-14282-X trade
ISBN 0-385-14283-8 prebound

Library of Congress Catalog Card Number 78-1213

for Sarah

Two girls made sleeping places on a swell of ground far from the homes of their families. They had been gathering roots for healing and in the morning they would return to their village to join other root gatherers in grinding and drying the roots for medicine. They sat close together on their little hill under the darkening sky and talked quietly of the sky dwellers.

"The old ones of our tribe say that every star is a person," said one girl. "How I wish I could have a star for my husband."

"That is a silly wish," said the other. "Such a marriage would take you far from our people to a land where you would not know anyone. I want to have a warrior for my husband and to live as the other women do."

"Still," persisted the first girl, who was more adventuresome than her friend, "I would have that star there, that brightest one, for my husband. Stars shine forever. Many warriors die young."

"Some do. Others do not. I will have a brave warrior who will live long and be as beautiful as any star." She rolled in her blanket and soon was asleep.

The girl who wished for a star husband stared into the sky until she too fell asleep. When she woke, a handsome man lay at her side. His young body gleamed and shone so brightly that she could hardly bear to look at him.

"Who are you?" she cried, and he answered, "I am your star husband. Few mortals are brave enough to make such a wish or beautiful enough to have it granted. I have brought you to the sky to be my wife."

"But where is my friend? How will she find her way home alone?" asked the frightened girl.

"A porcupine woke her and when she discovered you were gone, she followed after it. It will lead her to your village."

The girl was puzzled, but the young man's face and words were kind and soon she slept again, adrift in the night at the side of her star husband.

At first the great glittering sky delighted her. There everything stayed the same, or so it appeared to her mortal eyes. In the sky world, time was so enormous that it seemed to stand still. In the world she had left behind, time passed more quickly, and years on earth were as a day in the sky. For a long while, she was happy exploring her new home and enjoying the company of her handsome husband. In time she bore a son, who was the Moon.

Yet even with a baby boy to interest her, she became restless. Her husband was often away on the business of the night, and she was lonely. In the sky there was no need for cooking or weaving or any of the skills she had learned. She spoke to her husband about it.

"Star husband, I grow tired of having nothing to do. I would like to gather roots as I used to do at home. Are there roots here in the sky?"

"Dear wife, you must not try to go digging in the floor of the sky. Play with our son and tell him the stories of your people. But do not go digging."

Still she was bored, and one day as her baby son slept, she crept away and began to dig in the floor of the sky, using her fingers as a curved tool as she had done on earth. Soon she had opened quite a hole.

Suddenly, up through the hole came a wind different from the cold, clean air of heaven. It was a wind from earth, and on it were the fresh scent of green things growing and the pungent smell of animals. On the wind was the smoke of the cooking fires of her people and the sharp odor of the holy herbs used in ceremonies.

"Oh!" she cried and began weeping. "How lonely I am for my home. How lonely I am for the seasons, and for growing things, and for the warmth of horses. How I miss the old ones of the tribe and the young ones too. There is no place for me in this sky world. There is nothing here I know how to do and no use I can serve. At home I gathered roots to make my people well."

She went to find her husband and said to him, "Star husband, I must go home. You are a good husband to me, and I will miss you and our son, but there is nothing for me to do here. The sky has no need for a mortal girl."

Because he did not want to see her unhappy, the star husband told her she could go, but he refused to take her home. "You must find the way yourself. A wish can carry you away from home, but more than wishing is necessary to return."

"I will find a way," said the girl. She turned to where her son still slept. "Good-by, my Moon," she said. "You are a sky child and do not need a mother near, but I will watch for you every night."

As she walked toward the hole in the sky, the star husband called after her, "We will wait for you to come to us again, the Moon and I."

Carefully the girl began to unravel the woven hem of her gown. From it she made a rope, but she soon saw that she could unravel only a small amount, for if she used it all, she would be forced to return home naked. When the hem had risen to her knees, she cut the rope and dropped it through the sky hole. It did not reach the earth, but it hung next to a great tree. She made fast the end and began to slide slowly down. At the bottom of the rope, she kicked and swung until she was near a limb of the tree and then she grasped onto it and climbed the rest of the way down to earth.

Once on the ground she remembered the way to her village as she had seen it through the hole in the sky. She walked steadily and reached the village by nightfall. At its edge, an old woman sat stirring something in a pot. The woman was her friend who had followed the porcupine home. "But you are still young!" her friend exclaimed when they had greeted one another. "How is this so?"

"In the sky, change comes more slowly than it does on earth," replied the girl who had come home. "It is right for those in the sky but wrong for the people of earth. I have come home now to grow old as a mortal person should."

And grow old she did, gathering healing herbs and making them into powerful medicines for her people. She would marry no warrior and she lived apart from the others. In time she came to be known as Wise One.

Every clear night she sat out under the wide sky and watched for a glimpse of her husband and her son. In the face of the Moon she saw the baby boy she had left, and her heart reached for him. On cloudy nights she often dreamed of her sky family. One night she dreamed a song:

> In the sky
> I am walking.
> I am one
> of many stars.

She worked hard at her root gathering and healing. She watched the seasons change, the young things grow, and the old ones die. She knew it was the way a mortal was meant to live. Still, she longed for her star husband and for the Moon, her son.

One day when she was very old, she made a sleeping place and lay down in it, her face turned to the sky. When the women came, they found she had died. The people held ceremonies for her passing and in them they sang this song:

Then leaped up a blazing star from earth
up to the sky, where it shone in glory
good to look upon.

And indeed, she had gone in spirit to the sky. Free of her body, she had no need to stay longer in the changing world. She was ready to live in the sky with her son and her star husband. Often in the early evenings she can even now be seen, the first star to shine, close by the side of the Moon.

Jane Mobley is a talented young writer who lives in Kansas City, Missouri, with her husband and her baby daughter.

Artist Anna Vojtech lives with her husband and young son in the village of Knowlton, Quebec, Canada.